CAREERS

S

R

RIE THOMSEN &
TRISTRAM HOOLEY

E E

R

A

C

CAREERS

Layout and cover: Camilla Jørgensen, Trefold
Publishing editor: Karina Bell Ottosen
Copy editor: Heidi Flegal
Printed by Scandinavian Book

Printed in the EU 2025
1st edition, 1st impression

ISBN 978 87 7597 608 9 (pbk)
ISBN 978 87 7597 903 5 (e-pdf)
ISBN 978 87 7597 904 2 (epub)
ISBN 978 87 7597 905 9 (audiobook)

Published with the financial support of the Danish School of Education, Aarhus University.

This publication is based upon work from COST Action, Critical Perspectives on Career and Career Guidance (COCAG), CA23112, supported by COST (European Cooperation in Science and Technology).

COST is a funding agency for research and innovation networks. Our Actions help connect research initiatives across Europe and enable scientists to grow their ideas by sharing them with their peers. This boosts their research, career and innovation.

Aarhus University Press
Helsingforsgade 25, DK-8200 Aarhus N
unipress@unipress.au.dk
aarhusuniversitypress.dk

PEER REVIEWED

FSC www.fsc.org MIX Papir | Støtter ansvarligt skovbrug FSC® C010493

EUROPEAN COOPERATION IN SCIENCE & TECHNOLOGY

Funded by the European Union

CONTENT

NEVER FOLLOW YOUR DREAMS

THE RIGHT CHOICE?

In 2009, in an auditorium at Stanford University in California, a mature gentleman in a suit steps up to the podium. He is a professor, and he is here to tell the audience about his research on career development. After a moment he breaks the silence with these words: "Never follow your dreams," then repeats, "Never follow your dreams." In this room, already quiet before the distinguished professor began his speech, the silence is deafening.

European researchers in careers and career guidance cannot help but be fascinated by the country across the sea, often called 'the land of opportunity', where, we are told, people rich and poor have high hopes of successful careers. They may even envision themselves as the next Taylor Swift, Barack Obama or Elon Musk, since in theory American society gives everyone the same opportunities to fulfil their dreams, if they only work long enough and hard enough. In the nineteenth and early twentieth centuries such dreams spurred hundreds of thousands of impoverished immigrants from Europe to cross the Atlantic to take part in the race for a plot 'out west': A large tract of fertile land they could work into the basis of a life many times richer than the one they were leaving behind.

When John D. Krumboltz, a professor of psychology and education, stepped up to that podium, the realities of life were very different. By 2009, the 'American dream' had transmuted into the idea that in modern-day America, 'if you can dream it, you can do it'. Hence the deafening silence as Krumboltz opened his talk on careers by entreating his audience *not* to follow their dreams. But Krumboltz did not let his audience remain stunned. He went on to explain that young people preparing to choose a degree programme or moving into the early stages of their work lives are often encouraged to identify the field or activity they are most impassioned about, then do everything in their power to make it their livelihood.

However, Krumboltz went on, this only leads to problems. Recommending a person begin, and sustain, a career based on a dream that has been a long-held passion gives them a recipe for disaster. Instilling such career ambitions in very young people is simply too much, as it sets the expectation that their careers must also reflect and realise their greatest dreams in the future.

Krumboltz was presenting his reflections at a time when planning a career no longer meant following in your family's footsteps, as it did in the mid-1800s. Many novels have explored this once common experience. A good example by the Danish author Carsten Jensen is

Vi, de druknede (2010; translated into English as *We, the drowned*, 2012), much of which takes place on the small island of Ærø. Each and every one of the young men in the island's main port town, Marstal, either runs away to sail the seven seas or somehow works on or near the ocean. There is no question of career choices or realising a dream, since this was the only sort of livelihood they could imagine.

Even as the authors of this book on careers, we would have been very surprised if our school career guidance counsellors had asked us whether our dreams were to become professors of career guidance. Our responses would have been at best a resounding "no", and more probably complete incomprehension that such a job could even exist. The image of a professor was that of the physics genius Albert Einstein in his later years, with his untamed head of hair and white lab coat in front of a blackboard full of enigmatic scribbles.

In elementary school Rie was convinced she wanted to be a veterinarian; she was good with animals and did well in maths. Her high-school Danish teacher suggested she study rhetoric. When she applied for higher education, she submitted her programme priorities in the following order: 1) a teaching course in the rural south Zealand town of Haslev, 2) occupational therapy in the large southwest Jutland town of Esbjerg and 3) sociology in the capital, at the University of Copenhagen.

She was granted a place at her first choice, earned her teaching degree and loved her job. Then, after teaching classes in the last year of lower secondary - the

Danish equivalent of junior high school - she was offered a supplementary course to become a career guidance professional. She took the course and never looked back. Luck and chance also created opportunities and ideas that led her to the position she holds today, as Denmark's first professor of career guidance.

Tristram's earliest career aspiration was to be a cook on a spaceship. Children often have fantastical career aspirations of this kind, which don't necessarily map onto real jobs. It is not uncommon for young children to answer the question "What do you want to be?" with responses like "a princess" or even "a dragon", but as they get older they start to link their dreams with the world they see around them. This gradual drift towards realism is good, as there aren't many jobs as space cooks or dragons. But it can also be dangerous, as it means aspirations that lie outside your immediate social or geographical environment are difficult to maintain, increasing the likelihood that you will do the kind of job your mother or father did. As the British sociologist Paul Willis noted, this process is one by which "working-class kids" aspire to and get "working-class jobs".

As Tristram came from a middle-class family, his aspirations developed within that frame of reference. After studying English literature at university, he worked in a call centre, then wrote press releases for a telecommunications company, before heading back to university to earn a PhD in literature. This mainly taught him that he hated literature (more specifically, the study of it), and he drifted into various other jobs with no real plan, first into community history, then e-learning and then into career development. Maybe in this field he could make a life? After all, he would have to decide on something fairly soon: by this time he had a partner, a house, a cat and children on the way. Not because that was his dream, but due to a mix of luck (both good and bad), timing and the hope that he had found his way into a field where he seemed able to do well, and do good. After some progression upwards, with the support of a wonderful mentor and great colleagues, and various sideways moves, he ended up as a professor of career education.

Neither of our career paths followed a straight, logical trajectory from, say, late elementary-school dreams of being a veterinarian or early ideas of starship catering to holding chairs in career guidance. The same goes for countless other people. Indeed, it is probably true that such haphazard, unplanned and surprising careers are the most common. The British podcasters Sarah Ellis and Helen Tupper have named this phenomenon the "squiggly career", which we think captures it well.

Even so, we often ask children and adolescents, "What do you want to be when you grow up?" We're not simply fishing for answers like "a good person", "happy", "grateful" or "contented with my life". We want to know what they want to *do*, professionally, in their work life, as their job. This question is not normally designed to elicit answers about their wider life, for example whether they want to get married, have children, run a marathon or play the flute. The 'being' that we are enquiring about is primarily focused on the field of paid work; we would like reassurance that, even as a child, they have some kind of plan to move towards economic independence.

All young people must consider this question when deciding what to do after leaving school. At this point they are often confronted with the concept of the linear career pathway. This builds on the idea that people follow their dreams and plan their career steps logically and rationally. The dream of earning a specific degree and, later, getting a job to apply that degree comes to control the actions we must perform to fulfil our dreams.

You now know that our career paths looked nothing like this; they were much squigglier. This takes us back to that breathless moment during Krumboltz's talk about careers, when his words pierced the very heart of the American dream: "Never follow your dreams."

PLANNED HAPPEN-STANCE

Krumboltz coined the phrase "planned happenstance", a concept that seems to be an oxymoron: How can one plan for something to happen by chance? His point is that a person can plan to be at a certain place at a certain time - such as signing up for a degree programme, applying for a job or, on a smaller scale, attending a public celebration, a reception or a soccer match. We have no control of who else will be in our class, or who will eat a hotdog next to us at the celebration, strike up a conversation or cheer from the stands. But what we *can* do is put ourselves in more of these situations where we might meet people, have experiences and learn things. In other words, we can actively increase our chance of happenstance happening.

Then, when the chance arises, we can choose to react in different ways. If our gaze is firmly fixed on dreams that lie on the horizon, we may not see the opportunities a given moment offers. We may simply see them as noise, cluttering the path to our goal. Conversely, if we allow ourselves - or allow others to help us - to discover and investigate the possibilities happenstance offers, we may see a career we could never have imagined on our own.

According to Krumboltz, happenstance often affects our career development, yet we must not see random coincidences as regrettable mistakes or as deviations from our plans. This is too easily done, imagining that a career must follow a straight, predestined path.

Think back to our own stories, which, had we focused on mistakes and deviations, would have become stories of wrong choices - stories of how we failed to take the direct route. Of how, for Rie, choosing a career in teaching was a mistake, a waste of time, because she was 26 before she found out what she really felt passionate about - her real dream. In Tristram's case it would be easy to see everything he did up until his thirties as aimless wandering and wasted time, yet every day he still draws on the skills, experiences and relationships from that period.

When, early in life, the idea of a dream job becomes the ultimate goal, which all choices and decisions must lead to and bring to fruition, people all too easily end up castigating themselves for any deviations from the beaten, linear track. All we get out of this is frustration.

Another problem is that people can only dream of jobs they know about. We all develop as we interact with our surroundings, and a career as a veterinarian, cook, lawyer or politician, which once seemed like one's dream, may look less appealing several years later. In Rie's case, she is not even sure she would have had the stamina it takes to examine animals, not to mention operating on, castrating, inseminating and euthanising them. If, instead, we accept chance and perhaps even expect happenstance to play a role in our careers, this allows us to normalise the unavoidable deviations from our plans and use them to imagine what could be a future occupation.

As for future dreams, Krumboltz encourages people to test them by taking small steps forward, then being open to happenstance pointing in new directions. That is why the most important career-guiding skills, according to Krumboltz, are not making rational choices - laying out a plan or following it - but instead being curious and brave enough to explore unexpected opportunities.

This proposal may sound obvious to readers who have already experienced the winding, unpredictable turns a career can take. For young people, however, the expectations they meet as they finish their basic schooling make a big difference. Should they have a clear picture of their dream job? Be able to lay a plan to achieve it, and be resolute enough to take actions to follow it through? Or should they hear more about how educational plans and jobs often change? How happenstance plays a role, and how it is normal for lives to take a circuitous and, yes, squiggly path?

Unfortunately, across most of Europe and in many other parts of the world it is seen as a virtue and a duty for young people aged 15 or 16 to know what they want to study, and what job they want to land with their degree. One of the forces driving this trend is the somewhat unrealistic political ambition that young people ought to make the right choice the first time around. Yet people have a habit of changing their minds and learning from experience, meaning that what you want at age 15 may not be what you want at age 25 or 45. Furthermore, the labour market has a habit of changing, meaning that the job a person wanted to do at the age of 15 many not even exist 20 years later.

We want to emphasise that it is *not* wrong to dream about a certain career, or to lay plans and work to achieve one's goal. Planning is a useful skill. Still, a fixed and inflexible plan can tie you to your younger self's dreams, stifling your development and ability to take advantage of happenstance. It is worth mentioning that Krumboltz urges us to write our plans for the future in pencil - and keep an eraser close at hand.

OPPOR-TUNITIES ON THE HORIZON

GAME DEVELOPER BARBIE

From the moment we are born, we gradually adjust to the norms of the society around us. This process of socialisation takes place through family, schools, cultural meetings with other people, books, film and television, art and social media.

This means that children begin to form concepts of work and various professions in their society relatively early on. In our societies, children's books, songs and series are about Old McDonald on his farm, Postman Pat, the police pups in Paw Patrol and fire-fighting Smokie the Bear. Barbie dolls are sold with clothing and accessories reflecting various professions. According to the American toy company Mattel, Barbie has had over 200 different careers, including lifeguard, UNICEF ambassador, beekeeper, game developer and president. Countless popular television programmes show professional chefs, bakers, gardeners, financiers and interior decorators working their magic, or judging others who are vying for an apprenticeship or a place in the sun.

As they grow up, children's and young people's

imaginings about their futures are both inspired and constrained by the images and influences they see around them. Their imaginary future selves are influenced by the jobs they witness, particularly when these are performed by people from their own families or communities.

The British sociologist Louise Archer led the large-scale ASPIRES study, which investigated children's and adolescents' ideas and aspirations about their educations and careers. Archer and her research team have documented how children's career ideas develop over time. For instance, 10-year-old British pupils have a mainly positive perception of the natural sciences and associated jobs, whereas their perception of such careers is more negative at age 14, when fewer expect to choose a career in the natural sciences.

PAINTING A PRETTY PICTURE

Millions of people around the world have viewed a short motivational video, accessible on YouTube, called *Inspiring The Future - Redraw The Balance*. It features a class of young children in England who are tasked, apparently by guest teachers, with drawing a firefighter, a surgeon and a fighter pilot. The children set to work on what they clearly think is an interesting and engaging task. They talk about their figures and the names they give them, such as Firefighter Gary and Pilot Tom. When the guest teacher asks the children whether they would like to meet these people in real life, all hands go up: "Yeah!" Cut to the classroom door, through which step a surgeon, a firefighter and a fighter pilot in full gear. The surgeon is wearing shapeless blue scrubs and a hair snood, the pilot a fully visored helmet and a camouflage uniform, and the firefighter a similar helmet and a thick, dark-green uniform.

The two helmeted figures remove their head gear, revealing that they are women: the very 'guest teachers' who helped the class during the exercise. The surprise on the children's faces is manifest. "They're dressed up," one child blurts out.

Of the 66 children, 61 drew people in these occupations as men, while only five drew them as women. This video shows how children aged 5 to 7 have already formed gender stereotypes for certain jobs. The first version of the film was recorded in the UK in 2016, and the experiment was repeated in Denmark in 2020 using adults employed at the global shipping and transport company Maersk. This time the children were asked to draw a ship's captain and a chief engineer: 54 children drew male figures while only nine drew female figures.

Gender biases have a very early impact on the occupations we can imagine ourselves doing in the future. So does our belonging to certain groups, neighbourhoods, towns or regions, as well as our self-understanding and the expectations of the people around us.

People can only imagine possibilities they know about, and there are valid reasons why they might know nothing about possibilities that lies beyond their own horizons. It is hardly likely that a young man growing up in a disadvantaged suburb will know that there are training programmes he could take to become a dairy technician or a surveyor.

Statistically these are not professions he will encounter in his local community, nor ones his family and friends know about or might expect him to pursue. If, despite the odds, he becomes aware of these professions, he will probably not regard them as very relevant. They are not an option that lies within his horizon for action. As we have already heard, the combination of these assumptions about what is possible and a lack of awareness about alternative possibilities is what leads to working-class kids getting working-class jobs (and middle-class kids getting middle-class jobs, and so on). Put differently: 'You've got to see it to be it'.

An analysis by the Organization for Economic Cooperation and Development (OECD) - whose goal is to improve financial and social conditions for people around the world - has compared data from studies conducted in 41 countries to assess the knowledge and aspirations of 15-year-old pupils. It showed that adolescents have a relatively narrow perspective on the concept of a career, with some 40% of them focusing on the same 10 jobs. What is more, the group's focus narrows over time, meaning that even more of the older adolescents can only see themselves having a career within an even narrower range of jobs. The OECD calls this "career concentration".

FUNNEL VISION

In an influential study from 2006, the British education researchers Phil Hodkinson, Helen Bowman and Helen Colley investigated masters'-degree graduates' transition to the labour market and found that a narrow horizon for action also typified everyone in this group. Their conclusion supports the same point as the inspirational film: that our options and the possibilities we see for ourselves are related to our situations in society, our upbringings and our cultures. These three researchers therefore recommend that people become aware of their limited horizons and are supported in expanding them, for instance through career education and guidance.

The example of the English children aged 5-7 helps in understanding how socialisation ends up shaping perceptions of career development and possible opportunities, so that they resemble a funnel. The mouth of the funnel is wide, but it gradually narrows as we grow up and link our self-perception to gender, class and culture, and to our ideas about which jobs will bring social recognition or status. Eventually, our field of vision is so limited that out of the narrow end of the funnel we can only see an area that is much smaller than the mouth of the funnel. Simply put, we see fewer options.

Bill Law, a British career guidance scholar, has developped a theory about how people develop their careers. In Law's view, the crucial ingredient is a learning process. People need to learn about careers just as they learn how to clean, cook, build a house, splice genetic material or provide career guidance.

Working with the British researcher Tony Watts, as early as the 1970s Law developed what is now known as the DOTS model, which to this day remains a pillar of career education. The acronym stands for 'Decision learning, Opportunity awareness, Transition learning and Self-awareness' - elements that Law and Watts, and we too, regard as fundamental to people's ability to make career-related decisions.

Meanwhile, Law has since argued that it is necessary to develop the DOTS model to describe precisely how people can improve their ability to make career choices and decisions. The original DOTS model describes *what* we need to learn about our careers, but Law wanted to develop the model to show *how* we learn these things.

Law describes career learning as a skill with four levels. In the first level, children discover and sense the world in relation to the professions and functions in their local society. Note that Law's theory also considers how, say, a Western welfare society differs significantly from an Indonesian tribal society, meaning the professions and functions people discover will also differ.

If we think about a few different settings in which people might grow up, it becomes clear how our career learning is shaped by the world around us. A child growing up in Brooklyn, New York, is surrounded by a rich tapestry of small and medium-sized businesses, but they are also just a short train ride from the wealth of Manhattan - indeed, from Wall Street itself, which is arguably the centre of global capitalism. Career opportunities are everywhere, if the children can see them and acquire the education, contacts and personal capabilities to take advantage of them. On the other hand, for a child growing up in the Shetland Islands, which take a good 13 hours to reach by ferry from Aberdeen in Scotland, the range of opportunities is somewhat smaller. And what about a small Danish town like Billund, the home of Lego, which has one main employer - great for those who love Lego, but what about those who fancy something different?

Law's second level is where people begin to filter and arrange information according to their experiences. To any 13-year-old child, regardless of gender, the word 'surveyor' sounds both old-fashioned and extremely boring, although today this is a well-paid, high-tech profession with many and varied tasks. If teachers describe a 13-year-old boy as a good initiator, structured and responsible, the boy himself will hardly link these words to a career in nursing, even though these are core skills and character traits in healthcare professions.

At this level, then, people are at risk of erroneously sorting information. For instance, some people might conclude that a given qualification or occupation is unimportant or boring because their friends say it is. And sometimes others unwittingly fail to share vital information due to their own perceptions of jobs that are traditionally done by men or women.

Law's third level is about synthesising information and impressions of jobs and educational pathways, and placing each on an internal mental map of options. This map positions people, groups and events that are either actually or potentially important to a person's education and employment in relation to one another. This mental career map is used as people gravitate towards certain opportunities and, perhaps, try to avoid others.

The fourth and last level in Law's career learning theory is about being able to explain, anticipate and understand the actions it takes to make a career possible. Imagine a family in a small town who for generations have earned their living as non-skilled labourers. One reason for this may be that older generations hand down the narrative that schooling is a necessary evil, best dispensed with as quickly as possible. Members of this family would see no reason to ask about options for more education beyond junior high, but be glad to find a job as soon as they left school. Later in life some family members may meet others who also knew this pattern, but could explain that by meeting other people they had realised what it was: a pattern. Such moulds can be broken, then rebuilt in new shapes and colours, for instance by means of adult education.

CAREER AND COMMUNITY

Many people imagine career-building as an individual phenomenon, but if you think about it, you talk to others when you are making career choices, you take your family's wants and needs into account and you study and work with others. It is probably more accurate to think about career-building as an interactive social process rather than something that happens in one person's head. Once again Bill Law can help us with this issue, as he has identified five types of interactions between the individual and community that are important to career development.

First, the expectations - positive and negative - of other people are very important. It is not surprising that this is a recurring theme in numerous American films about high school.

The feature film *Freedom Writers* (2007) is based on excerpts from the writings of the American high-school teacher Erin Gruwell and her pupils. The school's expectations for these pupils are so low that their poor grades are a self-fulfilling prophecy. Enter a very special teacher, Gruwell, who demands of her class that they become something, become somebody. Their diaries speak about the racism and discrimination they experience, but also give them a way to tell their stories and write themselves into a new future which goes far beyond other people's limited and limiting expectations of them - thereby writing their way into a new place in the community.

Law's second and third types of interaction between individual and community are also illustrated in this film. The second is that we get feedback on our actions from others, and this shapes who we think we are and what we believe we can do. Gruwell provides her students with important feedback, both highlighting what their strengths are and calling them out on bad behaviour. Thirdly, Law emphasises the support - or lack of it - in our surroundings. You can't do everything yourself; sometimes you need to lean on a friend, a colleague or a teacher to move your career forward.

In *Freedom Writers*, Gruwell arranges a number of talks for her class by prominent speakers who also share their own stories. Several have personally fought to overcome prejudice. These scenes illustrate Law's fourth and fifth elements: the opportunity to access information about existing options, and to meet role models who can share their experiences and prompt people to reflect on the life and career options that might be open to them.

IF YOU CAN DREAM IT, YOU CAN DO IT

The danger of films like *Freedom Writers*, and indeed of any stories about how people overcome adversity and rise out of poverty and disadvantage, is that they can under-estimate real structural barriers. In Britain, there have been a total of 58 prime ministers since Robert Walpole in 1721. Of these, 20 attended Eton, an expensive private boarding school, and 31 studied at the University of Oxford. Looking at such statistics, it is difficult to conclude that Britain is a country in which talent, confidence and career aspirations matter more than one's social background and access to elite education.

Many studies of careers have investigated how so many opportunities continue to be reserved for the rich and powerful in seemingly free societies such as the US and the UK, and even in famously egalitarian societies like Denmark. No one says a person cannot become prime minister without having attended a private school.

Indeed, in recent years both Prime Minister Keir Starmer of the Labour party and Liz Truss, a Conservative predecessor in 10 Downing Street, were educated in government-funded schools. Nor is there any rule that a British prime minister must have gone to Oxford, or to any university at all. For instance, other, earlier predecessors, such as John Major of the Conservatives and James Callaghan of Labour, held no university degree.

Yet at every stage privilege works its magic, meaning that those from advantaged backgrounds are a little more likely to pass their exams at school, get into a good university, find a good job soon after graduating, get promoted in that job and so on. Sometimes we find evidence of actively discriminatory processes, for example when people who want to enter elite professions like the law, politics or the arts must work for free in unpaid internships. This is one clear barrier that serves to prevent those without financial means from accessing those fields.

Quite often, however, privilege works in more subtle ways. The French sociologist Pierre Bourdieu was the son of a postal worker, but he progressed to study at the École Normale Supérieure, one of the most prestigious higher education institutions in France. He found that to fit in he had to become more like his peers: the children of the elite. Being clever was not enough. He also had to lose his rural accent. This challenging experience of social mobility led him to reflect on the ways in which power and privilege work. Obviously, the more affluent have the opportunity to buy private schooling, work in unpaid internships and so on. But Bourdieu reasoned that not everything can be bought with financial capital, so there must be other kinds of capital that explain career success.

Bourdieu argued that aside from financial capital there was also symbolic capital (Do you have the markers of success, like a posh accent, nice clothes and a good address?); cultural capital (Do you share the values and tastes of those who are successful, such as enjoying Mozart more than Motörhead?); and social capital (Do you know important and powerful people who can help you to get ahead?). Because the different kinds of capital are interchangeable, someone who loses their wealth but has an elite accent and knows important people can quickly rise back up to the top of society.

The existence of what some call 'sticky floors' (alluding to the difficulty of getting unstuck from the bottom of society) and 'glass ceilings' (alluding to the extreme difficulty of entering its top echelons) means that social structures shape people's careers in all sorts of ways. This is not to say that people are unable to rise from humble beginnings to the top of society, as some of the young people in *Freedom Writers* aspired to do. Nevertheless, such examples tend to be notable because they are unusual rather than because they are normal. Given this, our careers can often become a process of struggling both individually and collectively.

A RACE OR A JOURNEY?

EVERYONE HAS A CAREER

The English word 'career' is rooted in *carraria*, Latin for 'race course', and most people probably do think of it as some sort of progression along a competitive track. Often the word is used in connection with successful people, frequently from the world of business, who have jostled their way to the top, as Jeff Bezos did at Amazon or Sheryl Sandberg did at Meta.

Taylor Swift offers an excellent example of someone who has built an amazing career, not only as a musician but also as an entrepreneur. She decided to change the type of music she played (from country to pop, then moving into other genres as well), to extend her audience and then to re-release her music to circumvent exploitative recording company practices, thereby actively building her own career and reshaping both her own life and the music industry. Swift even achieved global significance when, during The Eras Tour, economists noted that her concerts had an observable economic effect on the countries she visited. Clearly, very few can aspire to a career impact of this magnitude.

When, in conversation, we tell people that we are professors and 'careers' is our field of study, a common response is: "Oh, I don't have a career. I've just had a succession of jobs." Such reactions are based on the idea that a 'career' is associated with success, orderly progression up an organisational hierarchy, and social recognition and status - that a career is a ladder, and there is only one way to climb it.

Interestingly, we often use the expression 'career woman', but we rarely talk about someone being a 'career man', perhaps because it continues to be notable when a woman builds a career, whereas it is assumed a man will have a career.

Examples of career success are celebrated in the media every day. Sometimes they are highly predictable, as when the actor Dakota Johnson followed in the footsteps of her famous parents Don Johnson and Melanie Griffith (not to mention her maternal grandmother Tippi Hedren) and became a box office hit. Others are more surprising and recall the winding career paths and planned happenstance discussed earlier, as when the Danish writer and philosopher Morten Albæk became Senior Vice President of the international wind power company Vestas before going on to found, and serve as CEO of, Voluntās - a consultancy that specialises in meaningfulness. Some careers seem almost pre-ordained, while others are amazing acts of creativity.

Then there are those who have a unique talent in a field such as sports or music, which they turn into a professional livelihood. At the age of 45 the Danish skateboarder Rune Glifberg qualified for a place in the 2021 Olympics - making him the oldest athlete in a discipline included in the Olympic Games for the first time. The youngest athlete competing that year was Sky Brown, a 12-year-old girl representing the UK.

One common denominator in these examples is a career with high visibility in the media and the public sphere. This brand of success is, obviously, reserved for the chosen few, as opposed to the many who either unsuccessfully try to achieve similar goals or do not want a place in the limelight - although they would appreciate a good job. When it comes to fame and fortune, a career means recognition and status. However, in the field of career research we find other definitions that are more constructive and edifying, rather than reducing the overwhelming majority to losers in the career race.

Revisiting the work of Tony Watts, several decades ago he defined the word 'career' as describing a person's movement through education and work life. For Watts it is not a question of whether people build a career or not, or choose a career or not. Rather, it is a question of how the individual's career unfolds through their day-to-day interaction with others. In that sense, everyone has a career.

Watts's definition broadens the otherwise narrow concept of career, making it clear that this movement through education and work can take many directions and does not need to be an upward-moving process. A career can also move sideways, or turn back on itself. In this sense a career is less like climbing a ladder and more like tracing the cracks in a pavement of natural stone slabs.

Careers are about how individuals navigate the social structures around them, and make the most of the opportunities they are afforded. In seeking to understand careers we need to understand the perspective of the individual as well as the structures in which they live. It is rarely useful to use people like Jeff Bezos or Taylor Swift as models, but often very helpful to recognise that success means different things to different people. A choice that colleagues and friends may see as a step backwards in terms of pay, responsibility and recognition may be the exact opposite: a manifestation of a person regaining control of their own career, making their work life fit into the bigger picture of the life they want to live.

A COUNTERPRODUCTIVE UNDERSTANDING

One dark and drizzly evening in February 2020, Rie was getting ready to give an after-hours talk at an event for members of a trade union in the pharmaceuticals industry. The union had announced the talk under the heading 'What is a career? And do you feel stuck in yours?' The room was packed. The organisers had been obliged to limit attendance, so they decided to stream the talk online. Perhaps Rie of all people should have expected a strong turnout, but she was surprised. What did this large group want to know? And not least, what knowledge and advice were they hoping to get?

The first part of the talk addressed the question of what a 'career' is and what the word means. Initially the focus was on the conventional understanding of career-building as a linear progression through work, juxtaposed with the idea of a career being about making different aspects of one's life come together. The talk touched on other things we have already discussed, such as the horizon for opportunities, the influence of happenstance and how career shifts can emerge out of both crises and opportunities.

During the break a member of the audience approached Rie and told her that she had an advanced academic degree and had held several well-paid positions, but had never thought of herself as a person with a career. Yet listening to the talk, she had realised that everyone who has a job has a career. For her this realisation led to a sense of liberation, of having the freedom to explore and determine how the rest of her work life, and her life in general, should unfold.

To us, this exchange underscored the point that it *does* matter how we talk about careers and our career expectations. Perhaps the conventional understanding of careers is unproductive, or even counterproductive?

Here was a well-educated woman realising quite late in life that the concept of having or building a 'career' allowed her to think about her wishes for her own life, and to decide what to do about them. She recognised that she could affect her job options and life opportunities by proactively making educational and occupational choices.

Everyone has some power to shape their life and career. As discussed above, this does not mean that everyone can achieve whatever they want, nor that people should simply follow their dreams. Inevitably, we make career choices every day about how we spend our time and what direction we want to move in. Our Brazilian friend and colleague Marcello Riberio, also a careers researcher, has shared the story of José, a 36-year-old motorcycle courier with no formal education. Through a conversation with a career counsellor, José undergoes a process that is remarkably similar to that of the woman Rie met while giving a talk at the union event. José reflects on his past experiences, both in work and in his wider life, and recognises that he has made choices and built a career. This validates him as a person, and as someone deserving of a better life. His new awareness of his career empowers him to move forward in his life and actively develop strategies to improve his situation.

Of course, 'career' is not a magic word that can grant anyone a good life if only they speak it out loud. However, increasing both self-awareness and awareness of the structures around us can help us expand our horizons, which supports us in moving forward. Career education, counselling and other forms of support can be enormously beneficial by introducing people to these ideas and by helping them towards a breakthrough. Even so, too few people have access to career support services, and many dismiss them as being something that is 'not for people like me', in part because they view careers as an elite concept.

This understanding leads many people to regard a 'career' as something beyond their reach - a concept that is relevant to some and not to others. This in turn means that many people do not proactively think about their work life, telling themselves they have no influence on it.

They have a job, but perhaps not quite the job they want. They have interesting tasks, but perhaps those tasks drain their energy. Many people know the feeling of racing around in the proverbial hamster wheel without asking to be there - like taking part in a race without really knowing the rules, or what determines how many points you rack up on the scoreboard.

Bill Law contrasts the idea of "career as a journey" with the idea of "career as a competitive race". Too often careers are viewed as a race, with the only goal being to beat others and get to the finish line first.

Sometimes in a career context we do need to compete with others, for instance when applying for a job or a promotion. But the metaphor of the journey reminds us to involve ourselves in the experiences and opportunities we encounter along the way. We can be on a journey and make a stop to take part in a race, but we cannot be part of a race and take a time-out to digress on a journey. These two metaphors are helpful in drawing out different ways of thinking about careers. The narrow understanding of the "career as a race" entails an upward progression - the climbing of a ladder. This is the process only the chosen few can relate to, whereas the broader understanding of the "career as a journey" is about moving and travelling through learning, education and work life experiences. This journey involves focusing on the things we want out of life, and it encourages us to think beyond success in the workplace and reflect on how we balance all of the elements that make up a full life.

Concerns about the idea that we are all in an ever-accelerating career race has led some people to argue that we need to slow things down. In recent years, the 'slow work' movement has emerged to challenge the idea that work should be about frantic multi-tasking in pursuit of higher productivity and career advancement. Instead, slow workers emphasise quality over quantity, focusing on wellbeing, sustainability, purpose and meaning, and good work-life balance.

THE LIE OF THE LINEAR LIFE

When Rie took the chair in career guidance at Aarhus University, during her inaugural lecture in 2019 she conducted a brief experiment, posing three questions to the 300 people in the hall and asking for a show of hands. The object of this exercise was to do a real-life, real-time test of the traditional understanding of a 'career'.

First, she asked people to raise their hands if they worked in a field that was different from the one in which they took their first qualification or degree. More than half the people in the room raised their hands. Next, she asked to see who had had to acquire new skills when starting their first job, rather than having all the necessary tools from their education. More than half the audience had needed to learn new ways to work, and raised their hands. Her last question was how many believed that the grades from their diploma or degree had been decisive to their landing their first job. Of the 300-strong audience, about 10 people raised their hands.

Although by no means scientific, the result of the little test was not odd at all. The media show many examples of successful careers being an upward-moving phenomenon, whereas we rarely hear or read about people who make mistakes in their jobs, break the norms, take detours or live ordinary lives.

Politicians across the world typically have highly conventional expectations about young people's educational choices. The argument runs that it is critical for young people to choose the 'right' programme the first time around, then get their degree and a job that reflects the skills they have acquired. Preferably they should do this in a field that has a skills shortage.

Politicians often loudly express their views on which education programmes are 'right' and 'wrong'. Vocational programmes to qualify as a brick-layer or carpenter are currently being promoted in many countries alongside the call for more young people to opt for careers in care professions. On the other hand, politicians generally seem to consider an academic degree in art, drama or English literature quite useless. In the UK, politicians have frequently united with the media to denounce what are often described (without the permission of the Disney Corporation) as 'Mickey Mouse degrees'. However, when former prime minister Rishi Sunak pledged to get rid of such degrees in 2024, the politicians, the media and the higher education sector realised they could not actually agree on a definition of what a 'Mickey Mouse degree' was. The campaign was quietly shelved.

The question is: Will new social and economic developments prove the politicians right this time? Would young people be wise to plan their careers and focus on subjects that are more applied and obviously economically useful? One problem is that a series of reports by the British charity Education and Employers and the OECD have suggested that young people's aspirations are seriously out of kilter with the jobs actually available in the labour market. We agree that this is a problem and would argue for more and better careers education for pupils and students.

Having said this, recognising the value of thinking about what the world needs as you are developing your career is not quite the same as saying that everyone should dash into the areas with the largest skills shortages. Economists have a poor track record of predicting which jobs will dominate in the future, and the labour market has a habit of shifting and changing.

This could mean that the 80% of young Danes who do not pursue a higher education directly after high school may be making a smart career move. Taking time, reflecting and developing your life skills and experiences through travel, voluntary work, temporary jobs or short courses may actually be laying down useful foundation blocks for future transitions and flexibility. Perhaps we need to stop talking about young people taking a 'gap year' as if this was just an empty hole in their life. Far better, we believe, to think of this as a 'formative year', a 'year to see the world' or an 'experimental year' during which young people can develop and mature.

The prevailing political view rubs off on the young. Denmark's Centre for Youth Research's study 'Career focus in upper-secondary school' demonstrated how, in serious cases, the idea of 'one right educational choice' can lead to performance anxiety. It seems impossible to live up to political demands and expectations, not least because, unfortunately, the norms voiced by politicians do not reflect reality: A young person's choice of education and career is not simply a linear process, but often follows a bumpy, circuitous route.

One fallacy is the focus on 'right the first time' choices – since young people will be choosing paths several times as they move through the educational and work landscape. Blindly believing that young people must find jobs that are extensions of their qualifications or degrees is also meaningless – since any employee, whatever their job, must always be ready to learn new skills not acquired as part of their education.

On top of this lies the myth that really good jobs only go to those at the top of their class. Grades are only a part of what makes people successful. We have already introduced you to sociologists like Paul Willis and Pierre Bourdieu, who emphasise the role social structures play in shaping people's careers. Willis traces the way working-class boys "fight the system" by opposing school authorities and prioritising masculine values such as physical strength and humour, but he also shows how this ultimately, and paradoxically, leads these boys to accept and internalise their placement in low-status jobs. Being clever and being successful at school are not the same thing - but neither are being successful at school and being successful in your career. Besides education and class, there are a host of other factors that lead to career success, including attitude, personality, social and cultural capital, and just plain good luck (often helped along by a bit of planned happenstance).

Don't get us wrong: Education is important. We are both lifelong educators, after all. However, it is dangerous to assume that you need only work hard at school and choose your courses carefully to have a successful career. Careering is a far more complex, ongoing process, and no-one should think they have cracked the code merely because they get into a good university or land a good first job.

THE VALUE OF PRACTICAL INSIGHT

If politicians are misguided in trying to steer young people into certain courses and careers, the media are no more helpful to hopeful students choosing an education. Their platforms are full of stories that support the conventional understanding of careers as linear and progressing upwards, even when, under scrutiny, the examples they give do not follow this pattern.

We have already introduced you to Helen Tupper and Sarah Ellis, who wrote *The Squiggly Career*. They first rose to prominence following their TED talk, which was entitled 'The best career isn't always a straight line', reflecting in part their own decisions to step off the corporate ladder and embrace the squiggliness of their careers, which included shifting their work-life balance towards their family lives.

The Australian professor of career development Jim Bright has published a string of academic articles outlining a similar argument. Careers are not linear; they are 'chaotic' and 'complex'. Bright borrows the idea of 'chaos theory' from physics and the natural sciences to outline a "chaos theory of careers", presenting them as non-linear systems in which our psychology interacts with the social world in complex and unpredictable ways. This is a far cry from the career as merely a process of matching a person to a job. Careers are dynamic and always changing. This is illustrated by the following two examples, the first from the *Global Citizen* website and the second from *The Guardian*'s series about making 'a new start after 60'.

Esther Sunday was born in Nigeria, but she determined that if she was going to avoid getting married at an early age, she would have to leave. "I did not want to waste my potential," as she put it. Esther made her way to Europe via Libya, where she worked as a cleaner and housemaid for a Spanish family. Then war broke out in Libya and the family had to return to Spain. "They asked me to go with them," Esther explained, "but I was unable to leave because I did not have enough time to get a passport." From there she made her way to Italy and worked to integrate into Italian society, learning the language, finding a job with a government agency and volunteering in a refugee centre as a choir director. She also cuts and styles hair on the side to earn extra money. Esther wants to study more, and may even move to another country with more opportunities, saying "I am destined for far greater things in life. And I know I will accomplish my goals."

Our second example is Jane Swayne, who initially trained as a drama teacher, but then went on to work in dance therapy. Her values led her to found a charity that offered summer schools for special-needs children in post-war Kosovo. However, after a decade the funding for the charity was cut, and Jane lost her income. She decided to enrol on a course to become a chocolatier, turning what had been a hobby into the beginnings of a new life. This led her to found a chocolate business, where she still works at the age of 73.

Both examples describe exceptional people, and neither life story emerged as the result of a standard, linear career plan. Some people use the #twistedcareer hashtag on LinkedIn to make their squiggly career paths visible on a platform where most careers seem linear and upward-moving. Our hope is that readers of these stories will be reassured that straight lines are neither normal, nor necessarily desirable in our careers. The bumps and detours we experience along the way can have a positive effect, clarifying our sense of what we like and do well. Celebrating non-linear careers may help to make people feel less anxious about occupational choices - and taking vocational chances.

This is in line with the conclusions of the 'Career

focus in upper-secondary school' study mentioned earlier. As part of that project, several Danish schools did an experiment: They worked with pupils to develop more than just a 'plan A' for their careers. The very concrete outcome was that pupils felt calmer in the knowledge that options B, C, D or E could also offer interesting and desirable education programmes and jobs.

A LIFE IN FULL

RATIONAL AND IRRATIONAL CHOICES

In his book *SocioDynamic*, first published in 1998, the Canadian professor of counselling psychology Vance Peavy divides a person's life space into five different areas: learning/work life; personal/relational life; spirituality; health/body; and creativity/recreational life. In Peavy's thinking, mapping their life space enables a person to explore these areas one at a time along with their career guidance counsellor. Ideally, this joint investigation forms the basis of more insightful career decisions that consider more aspects of their life.

Peavy's approach is opposed to the 'rational choice theory', which is particularly applied by researchers in economics. This theory regards the individual as a rational decision-maker who can request information about an upcoming choice, list pros and cons and then make a deliberate decision, yielding the best and most useful outcome.

On the face of it, rational choice theory ought to make sense when people make career choices, especially when they affect their financial situations. The only problem is that many aspects that would be listed as pros in the work column of such a list would be listed as cons in the family or health column. Imagine an offshore wind turbine technician who travels 60 to 80 days a year. This might be a well-paid job that fits in with her skills and values, but this travel time is time she cannot spend with family members, in shared activities. In such a situation, what is the 'rational choice'?

This is how Peavy's approach and focus on the five life areas help us understand the complex interaction of career choices as part of our wider decision-making processes: At one and the same time, a rational and apparently 'right' decision in one life area can seem irrational in relation to other life areas.

THE CONDUCT OF EVERYDAY LIFE

In November 2020, Rie was sitting in her university office trying to find the time to write the original Danish version of this book. Meanwhile, she was simultaneously coordinating a construction project for a skateboard park in a small village in western Zealand. With a few other volunteers, she shared the task of making a communication plan. She was thinking about what to cook for dinner that night, as well as Christmas gifts, her personal exercise regimen, whether the gearbox of her car was disintegrating and where best to buy a compression-operated nail gun for her private construction project of transforming an old stable into lodgings suited to a teenager.

Rie is quite evidently a busy person who is adept at muti-tasking. Nonetheless, even she cannot be in two places at once. On this occasion she wrote to the publisher and asked if she could extend the deadline for submitting the manuscript. If we are using a conventional definition of a career, which focuses solely on paid work, we might see this as a career setback. Inversely, if we view a career as a balancing of all a person's different life areas, then we can reinterpret Rie's decision as a positive one for her career, which allowed her to organise a liveable life.

As academics we must learn to deal with peer pressure and keep our own ambitions in check if we also want to have a life beyond work. There are always more articles and books to write, but there is also more to life than scholarship. Other people's limits on career choices can be more structural. For example, imagine a healthcare worker with only the most basic qualifications who is keen to improve his skills, standing and pay at work. This person may have to decline an offer to study for certification as a nurse because it is impossible to combine family obligations and the family's financial situation with going back to school for several years. We all have choices to make about our lives, but sometimes even the most skilled careering cannot make life fair or get us everything we want.

Each day we must live our lives and organise our daily activities and responsibilities to manage different and occasionally contradictory demands. That is why a career path is not a set course we decide upon after spending four hours analysing our work-related preferences and aspirations. The paths of our careers develop daily, as we handle the many day-to-day choices we make.

CAREER AS CALLING

The two American psychologists Bryan Dik and Ryan Duffy describe a 'calling' in connection with work as a transcendent attraction to occupying a certain role in life in which we believe we can experience purpose or meaningfulness that lies outside ourselves - almost as if we are taking upon ourselves a certain vocation or life task without thinking of our own interests. We do this based on a strong inner conviction.

In a way, a calling is the opposite of a decision, as it comes before decision-making and basically replaces decision with fate. Fate is characterised by the absence of decision, in that events transpire and choices are made because they are intended by some higher power. This kind of calling is often associated with religion - we hear about people being 'called to the priesthood' - and for many people, faith and spiritual beliefs and practices can be a powerful influence on the career decisions they make.

The idea of being called to a certain walk of life or occupation, and the idea that external forces are decisive to the way we live, are evident in the English and German concepts *vocation* and *Beruf*. The Latin root of the English word is the noun *vox*, meaning 'voice', hence the verb *vocare*, which means 'to call'. Similarly, the German word *berufen* means 'to call upon', and also to 'appoint' or 'designate' for a particular duty or task.

In the religious sense, many believers consider a vocation to be a divine 'voice' calling upon a human being to carry out a certain obligation or task. We see this in the Old Testament, where God appears to Moses in the form of a burning bush, calling him to lead the Israelites out of Egyptian slavery.

At first Moses does not want to take on this task. Instead, he becomes afraid and tries to avoid his calling - a common reaction to religious vocations in the Old Testament, for when the Lord calls upon a human being to carry out a divine duty, this involves a huge personal responsibility for the fate of others, and much personal deprivation to boot.

For centuries many people also felt a calling to spend their lives as monks or nuns. They relinquished life with a spouse and worldly pleasures, dedicating themselves to charity and good deeds, and caring for lepers and the sick. Then, in the sixteenth century, a German monk named Martin Luther famously refuted the idea of being specially chosen and called by God to fulfil a sacred duty. No human being is closer to God than any other, he asserted, nor can any duty or religious action bring a person closer to God. His idea was in direct opposition to the Catholic Church and laid the foundations for northern Europe's transition to the Protestant faith.

In Martin Luther's view, when people believe implicitly their faith becomes visible through "the fruits of piety" - by which he means good deeds, mercy and benefiting others through whatever position, life or work situation we might have. The best way to believe, according to Martin Luther, is to apply ourselves humbly to the tasks of our station in life and act as well as we can to fulfil that role, benefiting our family, the state and the Church.

The German sociologist Max Weber has interpreted Martin Luther's concepts of calling and work as the foundation of a particular Protestant work ethic that paved the way for capitalist society. Weber argues that the capitalist focus on profit maximisation is an extension of the Protestant work ethic - although totally stripped of the religious aspect and spirit that are part and parcel of Protestantism.

The concept of calling can also be useful beyond its religious origins when we think about careers. People might feel 'called' to devote their lives to their country, to help others or to fight climate change. The sources of a calling can be multiple, originating from a higher power or coming from within, or from people around us. But when we are called, something happens that is quite different from rational decision-making.

The idea of a calling reminds us that our vocational, occupational choices can be justified on the basis of all five of Peavy's life areas, including values, spirituality and philosophy of life, rather than merely the amount on our pay check. What is more, the concept of vocation may make it clearer to us that we can gain inspiration and insights for our careers from both Google *and* God. While a search engine will yield information on various vocations, we also need to look closely at our values, spirituality and philosophy of life.

FEELING STUCK

WORK LIFE VERSUS REAL LIFE

Our work lives are unlikely to be exciting or fulfilling all the time. Sometimes we may experience our journeys through education programmes or jobs as tedious, even bordering on the intolerable. We may be stuck in jobs that looked like they were the perfect choice, yet now we find no meaning in performing our tasks.

Perhaps our work do not fulfil our needs anymore. We believe we have more skills than our employers are making use of, and to make the situation even worse, we cannot see any way to change the situation. The Swedish economist Torild Carlsson calls this being "burned stuck". The idea of being 'burned out' is well understood: Work overwhelms us to the extent that we are unable to function in our work lives and sometimes our personal lives too. Burnout has a sense of finality and crisis about it, while 'burned stuck' is more subtle, but potentially no less damaging. According to Carlsson, being 'burned stuck' occurs when our work aspirations and the significance of our work to our lives does not match the way our work lives are unfolding.

The term 'burned stuck' can be applied to various work life situations, but basically it covers a state of inertia in which the affected person cannot see how to move on or move out. And indeed, it is often difficult to put a finger on being burned stuck as we experience it, not least because for some of us, it is a taboo.

After giving an interview on this topic to the Danish daily *Berlingske*, Rie received feedback from numerous readers who shared their personal stories, enabling her to understand why the concept of burned stuck found such wide resonance. There were key account managers, preschool teachers, lab technicians, event organisers and bank advisors who all described finding themselves in this state during their careers. Many were able to look back and recall times when the phenomenon of being burned stuck very precisely encapsulated a difficult time in their work lives.

When we feel burned stuck, typically our first impulse is to quit our jobs and find new ones. However, it does not have to be like this, Carlsson explains. There is a good chance that we can get out of the burned stuck stalemate in our current positions. Carson notes that those who work in large corporations may be able to explore the internal labour market of the organisation. For instance, someone who is working as an accountant for the global corporation Price Waterhouse Coopers (PwC) may find they would get greater career satisfaction by working in the firm's 'Sustainability and climate change division', or they could become involved in the organisation's work on equality and diversity, or artificial intelligence, or even its charitable foundation. Very large companies, even ones that are strongly associated with particular sectors, are usually engaged in a wide range of activities and involve a huge range of different occupations.

After the *Berlingske* interview, a career counsellor told Rie about a woman named Lena, who for many years had wanted to work with tourists and events. But this seemed like an unlikely option for her in the contracting company where she worked taking customer calls, opening new case files, archiving and invoicing. She thought about asking to switch to part-time work so she could start her own event agency. Then, during a company event that was not going quite as well as her boss had imagined, Lena brought up her special interest.

This was not a conversation Lena had planned. Rather, it arose - in the words of Krumboltz - as planned happenstance while they were waiting in line at the buffet. Their wait was unexpectedly long because the caterer had run out of tartlets - a traditional savoury puff-pastry dish many Danes love. Lena spoke with her manager about the employees' food preferences and about her ideas of how such an event could have been organised.

Lena's manager could see the point in having more of the company's employee events being planned by the employees themselves, instead of paying an expensive event agency to do the work. He and Lena agreed she could organise the next company event during her working hours, and it was a great success.

What Lena managed to do is sometimes called 'job crafting', an often overlooked but extremely important career management skill. Job crafting builds on the idea that a job and its tasks are not entirely fixed. Over time every job will change, in aspects ranging from the very small to the quite large. We are often encouraged to adapt to our jobs by learning new skills and knowledge. In job crafting, however, we focus instead on how we can actively change the job to fit our needs. For the individual, this often involves focusing on the bits of the job you enjoy and reducing your focus on the bits you do not like. However, it can also mean suggesting new tasks you can take on, and which are a better match for your interests or values.

A FEELING AND A SITUATION

The Danish career counsellor Iben Treebak has looked at 'burned stuck' among mid-career members of the Danish union PharmaDanmark. Her aim was to gain a deeper understanding of Carlsson's concept of being burned stuck in a job by asking the members of the union to describe their experiences with what some researchers call 'mid-career stuckness'.

Treebak's investigation confirmed that union members experienced being burned stuck as a long-term, complex feeling of professional non-fulfilment, or of not having fulfilled one's career aspirations. She additionally found that burned stuck situations occur when people feel that their careers are virtually beyond their own control - when they feel subjected to general labour-market conditions they cannot control and may only be able to affect marginally and with great difficulty, even while being asked actively to address the issues at stake.

Finally, experiencing being burned stuck in a job was related to the conventional understanding of a career as a linear, upwards progression, which leads to clear but also quite narrow expectations about what a natural next step on one's career ladder ought to be.

One of the great challenges of feeling burned stuck is that it can be difficult for us to see how we got there. The feeling is somewhat vague, making it hard for us to describe the situation, which can have many different root and contributory causes. That is why both Carlsson's and Treebak's solution is to explore the feeling of being burned stuck, and our situation, in the most tangible sense: By digging deep at the spot where we stand.

Someone who is burned stuck must seek to answer several questions. First: What are my values, desires and goals, and my skills, characteristics and knowledge base? Then, after we have dug deep and found these in ourselves, we must dig deep into our workplaces to find out: What are my workplace's values, and what does it expect of me? According to Carlson, the root cause of being burned stuck lies in discrepancies between the answers we find in the individual and in the structures, for ourselves and for our workplaces. It is in the connections between these two views that we can see possible solutions take shape.

A LIFE-LONG CAREER

GAP YEARS FOR GROWN-UPS

In 1957 the American psychologist Donald Super wrote an article in which he argued that careers developed over a lifetime across five phases: Growth; exploration; establishment and consolidation; maintenance; and disengagement.

Super also formulated a series of life roles linked to the five phases: Child, student, worker, citizen, homemaker, leisurite and pensioner. Admittedly, when Super elaborated this theory in the 1950s the world looked very different from today, and many careers followed the structure he outlined.

At that time, work life and life in general - not least in America - was far more predictable. For one thing, there was less movement between the various layers of society. A maid's children would often become maids or doormen. A small-scale farmer's sons and daughters might get jobs at larger farms nearby. A doctor's sons would become doctors, which, incidentally, we still see sons and daughters of doctors doing today. Only the privileged middle and upper class pursued studies beyond elementary-school level.

Since then many scholars of careers and education

have criticised Super's model for depicting career as a phenomenon relevant only to a society's middle and upper classes. Critics also say his model is too narrow, describing only those who *take* jobs and not those who *make* jobs, like small businesses and entrepreneurs.

These days very few people spend their entire working lives in a single organisation or occupation. For some this simply has to do with frequent changes of jobs and employers. Research in the US on people who have recently retired found that the average person had 13 jobs across their working life, so it seems likely that those retiring 20 or 40 years from now might report even more. However, we now see trends that are reshaping the nature and length of working life altogether. People are typically in education longer and therefore start paid work later in life than their parents did. On the other hand, many people want to retire early, or at least engage in a phased retirement process where they work less as they get older. Others are interested in exploring the possibility of a leave of absence at some point in their working lives.

In 2016 the Danish pastor and author Poul Joachim Stender wrote a book entitled *Stop op. Fjumreår for voksne* - roughly translated, 'Take a breather: Gap years for grown-ups'. It was based on encounters with 55-year-olds who looked forward to living out various life dreams when they retired: growing apples, or travelling south, or relaxing in an olive grove. But as Stender asks: What if we don't live that long? Why wait till the final phase of life to live out our dreams?

Stender argues in favour of taking a year or two out in the middle of our careers to see whether we can make our dreams come true. Of course, not everyone is in a financial position to do this, but it is interesting that even those who can afford to take a gap year usually do not. The logic of the rat race is very strong. Getting out is seen as dangerous and counter-cultural, yet stopping to smell the roses could re-energise people and even make them better workers when they return (although increasing productivity should not be the only goal of our lives or societies). The subtitle of Stender's book - 'gap years for grown-ups' - also invites readers to imagine taking up academic studies again and reminds them that the possibilities of their youth might still be available.

Taking a gap year or two as an adult could even result in a whole different career from the one you had before. Changing track might offer new opportunities, resulting in what some call 'serial career-building' - where, over a long lifetime, a career can offer several different types of work. Flemming Rosleff is a good example, and a very well-known one across Denmark. After his first career as a medical doctor he became the director of a large private clinic, then moved on to a position as a check-out worker in a Copenhagen supermarket chain, ultimately being voted "Nicest Check-Out Lady of the Year" by readers of the weekly home-maker's magazine *Hjemmet*. Similar career moves have also taken former CEOs to new careers, for instance as park officers in Tivoli, the world-famous Danish amusement park in central Copenhagen. Common to their stories of serial career-building is the wish to leave a hectic work life with heavy responsibilities, replacing it with a meaningful work life that is less burdensome.

Often, however, a person's career will take a course of its own, without much rumination. This means - fortunately - that there are questions we are not obliged to consider every day. Having said that, subjecting our careers to a service check every now and then is always healthy. And speaking of health, we can become ill or experience pressures that force us to reconsider the career paths we had planned.

BREAKING THE SOCIAL CONTRACT?

In a research project Rie did in 2014 with colleagues Pia Cort and Kristina Mariager-Anderson, working with numerous other international colleagues, people from across Europe submitted accounts of their career changes following a health crisis or period of illness. Our interviewees spoke of how their workplaces, the health system, case workers, family, friends and former colleagues were initially quite intent on their getting back into the same type of job that had either made them ill or made them want to leave it, but then often changed their mind. The two stories we relate below are inspired by this research and exemplify how a radical career change can suddenly become necessary.

Hannah, a preschool teacher, was leaving a roundabout while driving to work, taking the same route she had taken for many years. Suddenly she was thrust toward the car's windshield, but the airbag was activated and her head was knocked back against the headrest of the driver's seat. A car had rammed her from behind at high speed. At the hospital the doctor found that she had suffered a whiplash injury, and she was discharged to recover at home.

Ivor was starting up his PC to prepare his closing arguments in a parental custody case. He had done this many times before, often under pressure. Sometimes feeling pressed for time even made him feel invincible, invigorated, as if some constant energy source just kept him going. His calendar was brimming with lots of exciting jobs. An hour later his partner in the law firm walked into his office and found him on the floor weeping, unable to recall how he had ended up there. His partner called an ambulance.

Hannah and Ivor share the circumstance that unforeseen events made them unable to handle the job they had before they became ill. They had to make radical career changes, but they did not yet know that research indicates this process takes time.

The study showed that radical career change is an extremely demanding process in terms of individual will power and tenacity. We could also conclude that none of the participating countries have very good support structures in place for this type of 'career U-turn'. The reason is simple: If publicly financed at all, the task of offering career guidance is spread among many different actors and is therefore often completely invisible to potential users.

There are some countries that offer stronger adult guidance services, although none are perfect. We would highlight countries like the Netherlands, Finland and Norway as offering a wide range of guidance services to adults - services that are actually taken up by a sizable proportion of the population. Norway, for example, has set up 28 career centres across the country, staffed with careers professionals capable of offering all citizens a 360-degree career check. These services are available to everyone, whether they are going at full speed, experiencing a period of stuckness or feeling lost in terms of direction, or have fallen ill and out of employment altogether.

The patchy levels of entitlement to career guidance for adults is strange, in part because we make most of our career decisions while we are adults, yet most career support is provided during childhood and adolescence. There would be considerable value in giving people better access to career guidance, both for their own wellbeing and for the effective functioning of society. Ronald Sultana, a Maltese professor of sociology of education, argued that we should view career guidance as an essential part of the 'social contract' that exists between citizens and their government. The state should make sure that citizens can maintain a certain standard of living, even in times of unemployment or illness, whereas inversely, citizens should be willing to work and contribute to society. Career guidance can make this contract a reality by helping people find out about what society needs and manage the ups and downs we all inevitably experience in our careers.

A PERSONAL CONSTRUCTION PROJECT

In 2020, the Danish age researcher Henning Kirk published a book entitled *Godt nyt om gamle hjerner. Om hjernens livskarriere og voksenlivets vækstmuligheder* ('Good news about old brains: On the brain's life career and the growth opportunities in adulthood'). Kirk uses the phrase 'life career' because he wants to encourage us to see our brains as a lifelong "personal construction project we are rebuilding, refurbishing, adding, breaking down and restoring, with all this taking place simultaneously - and very individually - depending on impacts of a long life on this organ."

According to Kirk, age research has been suffering from teething troubles for some years, resulting in seniors being treated as a uniform group and with a lot of bias linked to what he calls the "late-life career". One bias is that all seniors have difficulty remembering. Well, yes, Kirk says, they do. On the other hand, many senior brains have built a capability for analytical and strategic thinking that stems from combining previous experiences with new solutions. Kirk calls this "late-life competence", pointing it out as a strong card in the hands of senior employees, including those with short-term memory issues.

In the same way, the term 'life career' may help us to understand and exploit the fact that every person's career is a lifelong individual construction project of simultaneous rebuilding, refurbishing, adding, breaking down and restoration. The term embodies both the width and the long-term perspective of this imagery.

Such a perspective creates the opportunity to consider where and how we, as people, find ways to channel our capacities, also in transitioning from the labour market to other activities in life that may not be paid but can still be regarded as useful work. In some cases such work may be even more useful than the work we do to earn money. For instance, older people are often the backbone of charities, voluntary associations and civic life, but they rarely get paid for this essential social contribution.

FIVE TIPS FOR THE ROAD

Internet sites, magazines and professional journals often offer useful, well-intentioned tips on how to career. The vast majority focus on what each individual can do, thereby subscribing to a limited and conventional idea of careers as a kind of competition.

Usually scholars do not join the chorus giving advice. However, since this book represents an attempt to broaden interest in the concept of careers, it seems only right and proper to offer readers a few tips. We recommend that everyone sees their career as a journey through life, learning and work that they make with other people, during which chance and opportunity, often limited by the social structures around them, will surely play a role.

First and foremost, we ought to see our careers more

broadly. A career is not merely an education followed by a job. Rather, it is a journey through life, in which we interact with others and with the wider world - and it is much more than just what happens in our workplace.

Second, we must remember that there is nothing wrong with us when we fail to thrive in a job or educational setting. We may have a bad employer, the wrong job or too much to do, but we are exactly who we are supposed to be. Of course, this does not mean we cannot learn from our mistakes and setbacks. These are, indeed, often the best teachers. So if we find ourselves in career predicaments, we can reconsider and reflect on our situations, ourselves, our values and our ways of working and think about new ways to approach things in the future. But, we should avoid blaming ourselves for problems that may be beyond our control.

Our third tip is: Be willing to challenge the way things are organised in your life and your workplace if they are unfair or do not work for you. We do not always have to bow to demands that *we* should change, adapt or conform. Our employer may think we are the ones who have to change, but in some circumstances it may be the company's perspective on its employees that needs a rethink. This is not to say that all change is bad, but rather to note that it is not necessarily good. The problem is that when we start trying to change things in our workplace, we will probably need a little help. That is why, if you do this, you will often need to investigate collective options for changing your workplace or educational setting. When people come together, they have a much greater chance of influencing situations in ways that allow their careers to flourish.

Fourthly, we believe it is important to build a mental map which recognises that your career is a landscape with hills and valleys. We will inevitably experience highs and lows in our careers, and this is normal, but just because you are in a valley right now does not mean you will not be back on a mountain summit next year. We must remind ourselves and each other that no one can see what is hidden behind the horizon. And when we stray and lose our bearings, or when we feel stuck, we can seek career guidance to once again find our footing in the hilly, windswept landscape.

Fifth and finally, remember that although you do have some control over your career, you cannot control everything. Here, we are reminded of the American theologian Reinhold Niebuhr, credited as the originator of what later, in various wording, became widely known as the Serenity Prayer: "God, give us grace to accept with serenity the things that cannot be changed, courage to change the things which should be changed, and the wisdom to distinguish the one from the other." This a good maxim to keep in mind as you make your way through your career.

Most importantly, we recommend that you enjoy the ride through life as much as you can, and be ambitious about the ways in which you mould your own career to shape it into what you want it to be.